ESL Phonics for All Ages

Book 3

Consonant Clusters

Elizabeth Claire

Illustrations by

Dave Nicholson

Illustrations: Dave Nicholson
Developmental Editor: Nancy Baxer
Copy Editors: Nadine Simms, Samantha Coles
Fumie Fukushima,
Tina DiBella, Adelaide Coles
Layout: Robert Metz
Cover Photo: Corbis Photos

©2010 Elizabeth Claire
Published by: Eardley Publications
Virginia Beach, Virginia
Elizabethclaire.com

Printed in the United States of America

ISBN: 978-0937630-15-0

0 1 2 3 4

Contents

Book 3: Consonant Clusters

To the teacher: Each unit presents three to six consonant clusters with illustrations of common examples for vocabulary development and auditory and visual recognition. The consonants are then contrasted. A conversation or a song with high-frequency words is included in each unit for memorization and sight reading. Answer pages, a teacher's guide, and two audio CDs for this book are available.

👂 Listen, 🗣 Say, and ✏ Write

These words begin with the sounds /cl/.

👂 Listen to the words.   🗣 Say the words.

✏ Write **cl** at the beginning of these words.

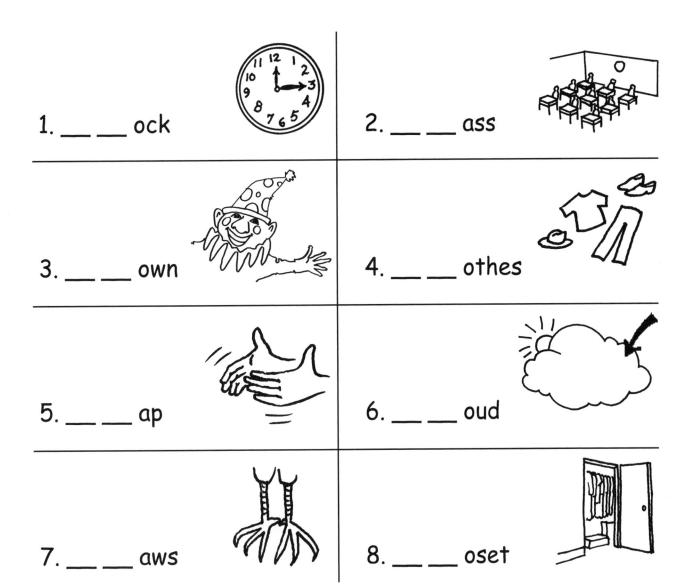

1. __ __ ock

2. __ __ ass

3. __ __ own

4. __ __ othes

5. __ __ ap

6. __ __ oud

7. __ __ aws

8. __ __ oset

👂 Listen, 🗣 Say, and ✏ Write

These words begin with the sounds /fl/.

👂 Listen to the words. 🗣 Say the words.

✏ Write fl at the beginning of these words.

1. __ __ ag

2. __ __ y

3. __ __ ower

4. __ __ oor

5. __ __ ea

6. __ __ ute

7. __ __ ood

8. __ __ ame

ESL Phonics for All Ages Book 3 • © Elizabeth Claire, Inc. 2008

👂 Listen, 😺 Say, and ✏ Write

These words begin with the sounds /pl/.

👂 Listen to the words. 😺 Say the words.

✏ Write **pl** at the beginning of these words.

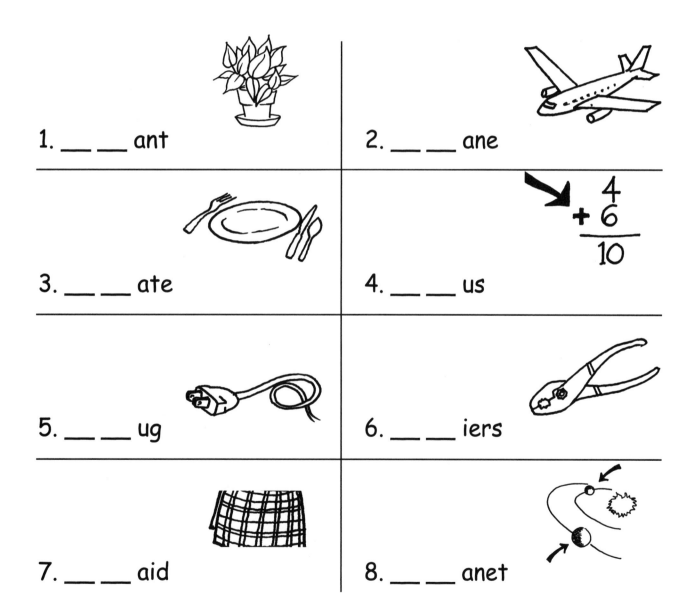

1. __ __ ant

2. __ __ ane

3. __ __ ate

4. __ __ us

5. __ __ ug

6. __ __ iers

7. __ __ aid

8. __ __ anet

UNIT 1

7

Listen, Say, and Write

Listen to the words. Say the words.

Write **cl, fl, or pl**.

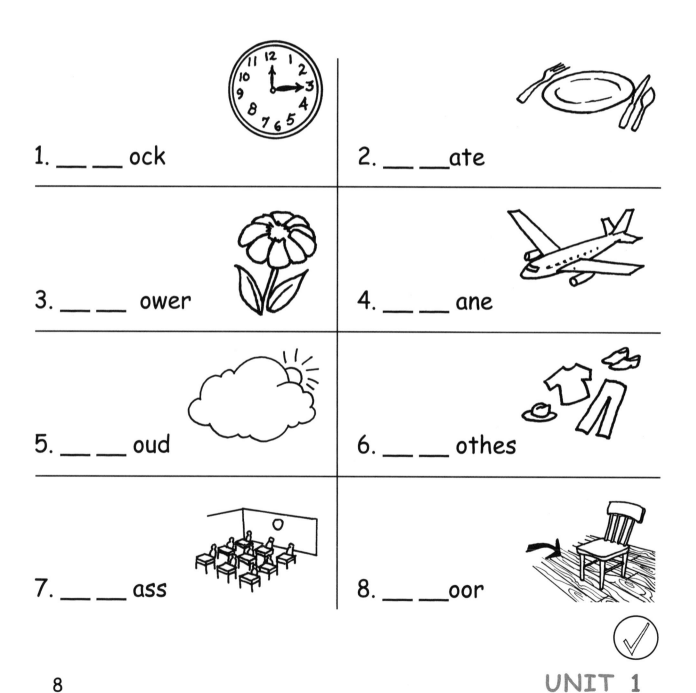

1. __ __ ock

2. __ __ate

3. __ __ ower

4. __ __ ane

5. __ __ oud

6. __ __ othes

7. __ __ ass

8. __ __oor

UNIT 1

Read, Find, and Circle

 Read the words.

Find two words that are the same.

Draw a circle around the two words.

1. pant   (plant)   plate   plan   (plant)

2. clap   chap   clap   cap   lap

3. floor   flood   for   flood   food

4. crock   sock   lock   clock   clock

5. clown   crowd   cloud   clown   could

6. flea   fry   fly   for   fly   ✓

UNIT 1

9

👓 Look, 👂 Listen and 🔍 Find

👓 Look at the pictures. 👂 Listen to the sentences.

 Find the correct sentence.

1.

    (a. Please pass the plate.)

    b. Please clap for the clown.

2.

    a. Please fly the plane.

    b. Please close the closet.

3.

    a. Please clean the clothes.

    b. Please sleep on the floor.

4.

    c. Please play the flute.

    d. Please pay for the clock.

10   UNIT 1

Listen, Read, and Sing

If You're Happy
and You Know It

If you're happy and you know it,
Clap your hands!

If you're happy and you know it,
Clap your hands!

If you're happy and you know it,
And you really want to show it,

If you're happy and you know it,
Clap your hands!

UNIT 1

11

👂 Listen, 🐜 Say, and ✏️ Write

These words begin with the sounds /bl/.

👂 Listen to the words. 🐜 Say the words.

✏️ Write **bl** at the beginning of these words.

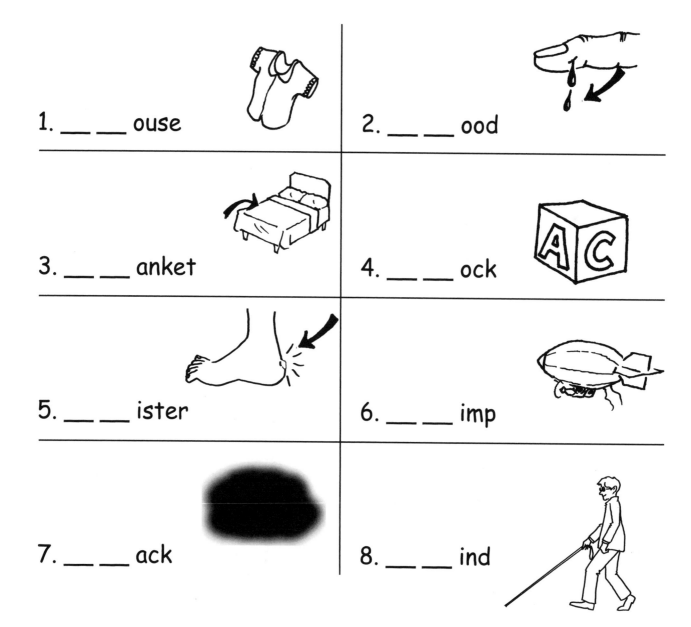

1. __ __ ouse

2. __ __ ood

3. __ __ anket

4. __ __ ock

5. __ __ ister

6. __ __ imp

7. __ __ ack

8. __ __ ind

UNIT 1

ESL Phonics for All Ages Book 3 · © Elizabeth Claire, Inc. 2008

👂 Listen, 🐞 Say, and ✏ Write

These words begin with the sounds /gl/.

👂 Listen to the words. 🐞 Say the words.

✏ Write **gl** at the beginning of these words.

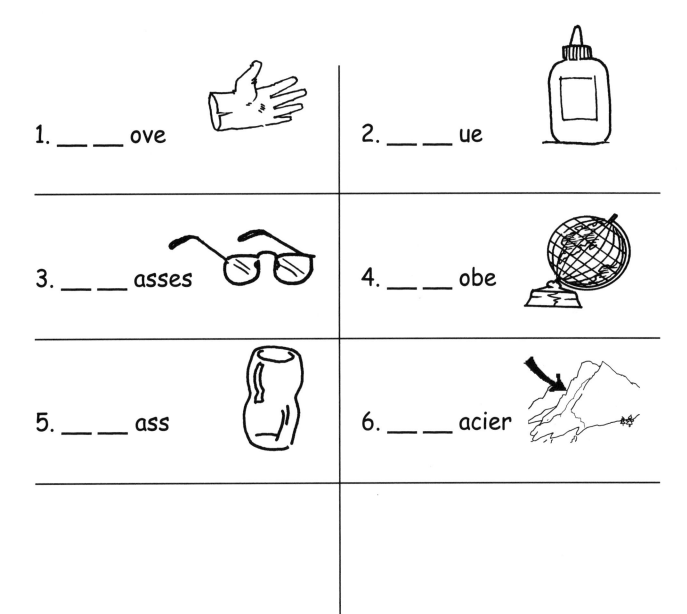

1. __ __ ove

2. __ __ ue

3. __ __ asses

4. __ __ obe

5. __ __ ass

6. __ __ acier

👂 Listen, 🐜 Say, and ✏️ Write

These words begin with the sounds /sl/.

👂 Listen to the words. 🐜 Say the words.

✏️ Write **sl** at the beginning of these words.

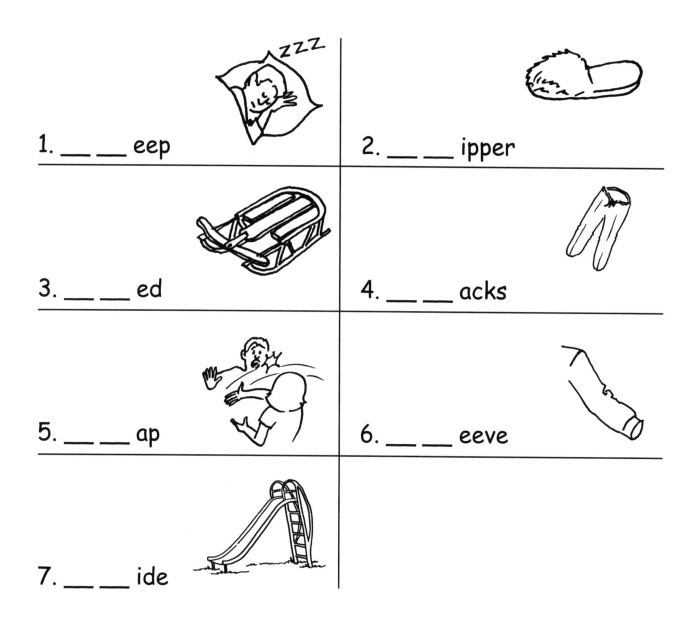

1. __ __ eep

2. __ __ ipper

3. __ __ ed

4. __ __ acks

5. __ __ ap

6. __ __ eeve

7. __ __ ide

UNIT 1

👂 Listen, 🐝 Say, and ✏️ Write

👂 Listen to the words. 🐝 Say the words.

✏️ Write **bl**, **gl**, or **sl** at the beginning of the words.

1. __ __ ove

2. __ __ eeve

3. __ __ eep

4. __ __ ouse

5. __ __ asses

6. __ __ ipper

7. __ __ ock

8. __ __ anket

UNIT 1

📖 Read, 🔍 Find, and ✏ Circle

📖 Read the words.

🔍 Find two words that are the same.

✏ Draw a circle around the two words.

1. block	blouse	glass	globe	blouse

2. blimp	blimp	slipper	slap	glint

3. glass	globe	glove	globe	grass

4. sleeve	slide	sleep	slip	sleep

5. slap	sled	slacks	slap	slit

6. blood	plate	plane	blind	plane

16

UNIT 1 ✓

👂 Listen, 🗣 Say, and ✏ Write

These words begin with the sounds /cr/.

👂 Listen to the words.　🗣 Say the words.

✏ Write **cr** at the beginning of these words.

1. __ __ y

2. __ __ ayons

3. __ __ ib

4. __ __ ab

5. __ __ own

6. __ __ owd

7. __ __ ow

8. __ __ oss

◯ Listen, 🐛 Say, and ✏ Write

These words begin with the sounds /fr/.

◯ Listen to the words. 🐛 Say the words.

✏ Write **fr** at the beginning of these words.

1. __ __ og

2. __ __ actions $\frac{1}{8}$ $\frac{2}{5}$

3. __ __ iends

4. __ __ uit

5. __ __ ame

6. __ __ ozen

7. __ __ y

8. __ __ iday

UNIT 2

👂 Listen, 🗣 Say, and ✏ Write

These words begin with the sounds /pr/.

👂 Listen to the words.   🗣 Say the words.

✏ Write **pr** at the beginning of these words.

1. __ __ ize

2. __ __ ice

3. __ __ ince

4. __ __ une

5. __ __ ison

6. __ __ esent

7. __ __ etzel

8. __ __ ay

👂 Listen, 🗣 Say, and ✏ Write

👂 Listen to the words. 🗣 Say the words.

✏ Write **cr**, **fr**, or **pr** at the beginning of the words.

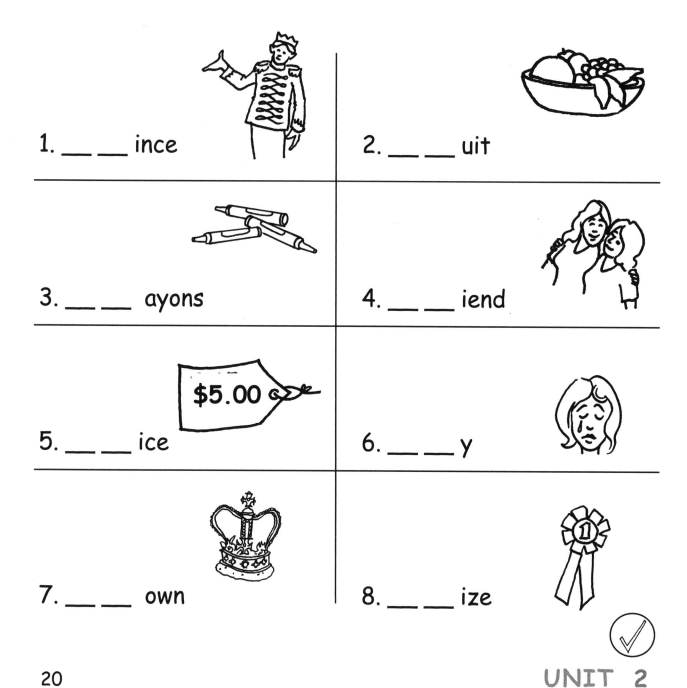

1. __ __ ince

2. __ __ uit

3. __ __ ayons

4. __ __ iend

5. __ __ ice

6. __ __ y

7. __ __ own

8. __ __ ize

UNIT 2

📖 Read, 🔍 Find, and ✏️ Circle

 Read the words.

 Find two words that are the same.

✏️ Draw a circle around the two words.

1. price   prince   prize   prince   please

_____

2. fruit   fruit   friend   fiend   fried

_____

3. clown   crown   crow   crown   cry

_____

4. present   pretzel   prison   present   prize

_____

5. crib   crab   cry   crayons   crab

_____

6. Friday   fry   fly   fruit   fry

✓

👂 Listen, 🗣 Say, and ✏️ Write

These words begin with the sounds /br/.

👂 Listen to the words.   🗣 Say the words.

✏️ Write **br** at the beginning of these words.

1. __ __ ead

2. __ __ ush

3. __ __ ick

4. __ __ ain

5. __ __ anch

6. __ __ oom

7. __ __ idge

8. __ __ aids

ESL Phonics for All Ages Book 3 · © Elizabeth Claire, Inc. 2008

👂 Listen, 🗣 Say, and ✏ Write

These words begin with the sounds /dr/.

👂 Listen to the words. 🗣 Say the words.

✏ Write **dr** at the beginning of these words.

1. __ __ ess

2. __ __ um

3. __ __ aw

4. __ __ awer

5. __ __ ive

6. __ __ eam

7. __ __ agon

8. __ __ apes

👂 Listen, 🗣 Say, and ✏ Write

These words begin with the sounds /gr/.

👂 Listen to the words. 🗣 Say the words.

✏ Write **gr** at the beginning of these words.

1. __ __ andmother

2. __ __ apes

3. __ __ ass

4. __ __ andfather

5. __ __ aduate

6. __ __ ave

7. __ __ apefruit

8. __ __ aph

Listen, Find, and Circle

Listen to the word.

Find two words that are the same.

Draw a circle around the same words.

1. brush	bush	rush	brush	bridge

2. bed	bread	read	bread	brown

3. crab	crowd	crown	crown	crayons

4. boom	broom	room	brown	broom

5. glass	grass	grapes	grass	class

6. price	prince	prize	pliers	prince

UNIT 2

25

© Elizabeth Claire, Inc. 2008 · ESL Phonics for All Ages Book 3

👂 Listen, 🗣 Say, and ✏ Write

👂 Listen to the words.   🗣 Say the words.

✏ Write **br**, **dr**, or **gr** at the beginning of the words.

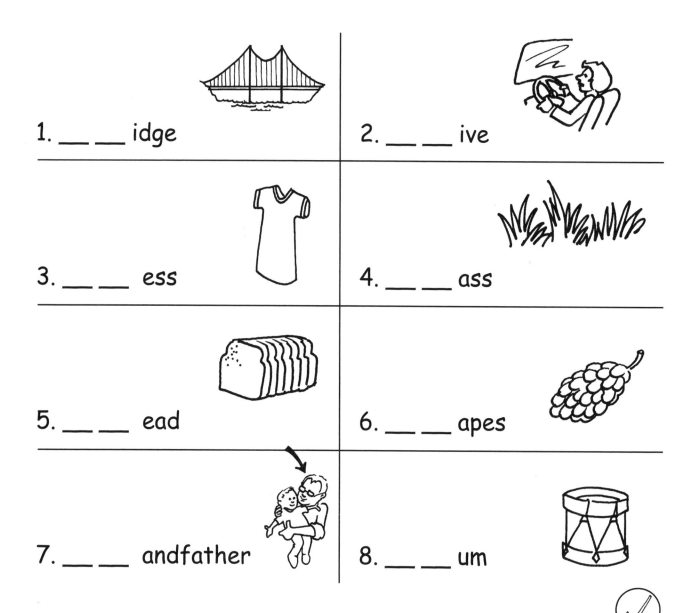

1. __ __ idge

2. __ __ ive

3. __ __ ess

4. __ __ ass

5. __ __ ead

6. __ __ apes

7. __ __ andfather

8. __ __ um

✓

UNIT 2

Are You Sleeping?

Are you sleeping?
Are you sleeping?

Brother John?
Brother John?

Morning bells are ringing,
Morning bells are ringing,

Ding ding dong!
Ding ding dong!

 Listen, Say, and Write

Listen to the words. Say the words.

Write **cl**, **cr**, **fl**, **fr**, **gl**, or **gr**.

1. __ __ oud

2. __ __ owd

3. __ __ y

4. __ __ y

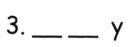

5. __ __ ass

6. __ __ ass

7. __ __ ute

8. __ __ uit

ESL Phonics for All Ages Book 3 · © Elizabeth Claire, Inc. 2008

UNIT 2

👓 Look, 👂 Listen and 🔍 Find

👓 Look at the pictures. 👂 Listen to the sentences.
🔍 Find the correct sentence.

1.   a. The frog is frozen.

     (b. The crayons are broken.)

2.   a. A fish is frying.

     b. A plane is flying.

3.   a. She's driving a car.

     b. She's bringing a broom.

4.   a. He's cleaning a glass.

     b. He's crossing the road.

UNIT 2

29

👂 Listen, 🗣 Say, and ✏ Write

👂 Listen to the words. 🗣 Say the words.

✏ What are the beginning sounds?

Write **br, cr, dr, fr, gr,** or **pr**.

1. __ __ ound	2. __ __ ize	3. __ __ ink
4. __ __ iend	5. __ __ y	6. __ __ y
7. __ __ andmother	8. __ __ own	9. __ __ ush
10. __ __ ain	11. __ __ own	12. __ __ een
13. __ __ ayons	14. __ __ og	15. __ __ ince
16. __ __ um	17. __ __ ass	18. __ __ uit
19. __ __ ive	20. __ __ ess	21. __ __ other

30

UNIT 2

👂 Listen, 🗣 Say, and ✏ Write

👂 Listen to the words.

🗣 Say the words.

✏ Write **st** at the beginning of these words.

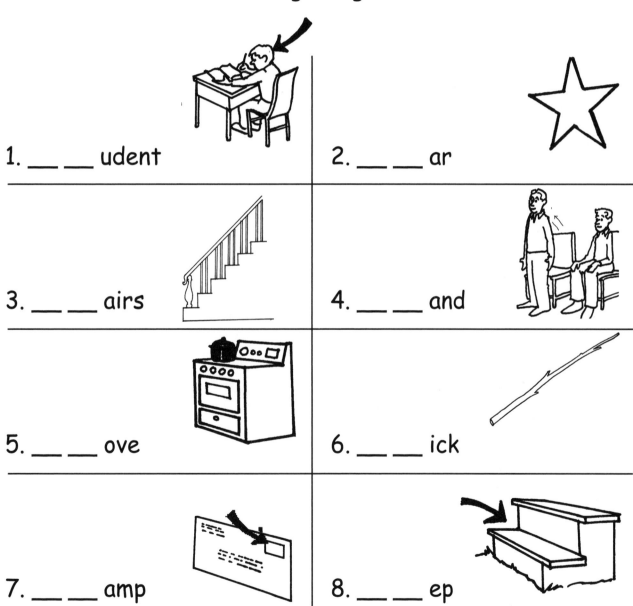

1. __ __ udent

2. __ __ ar

3. __ __ airs

4. __ __ and

5. __ __ ove

6. __ __ ick

7. __ __ amp

8. __ __ ep

👂 Listen, 🕷 Say, and ✏ Write

👂 Listen to the words.

🕷 Say the words.

✏ Write **sp** at the beginning of these words.

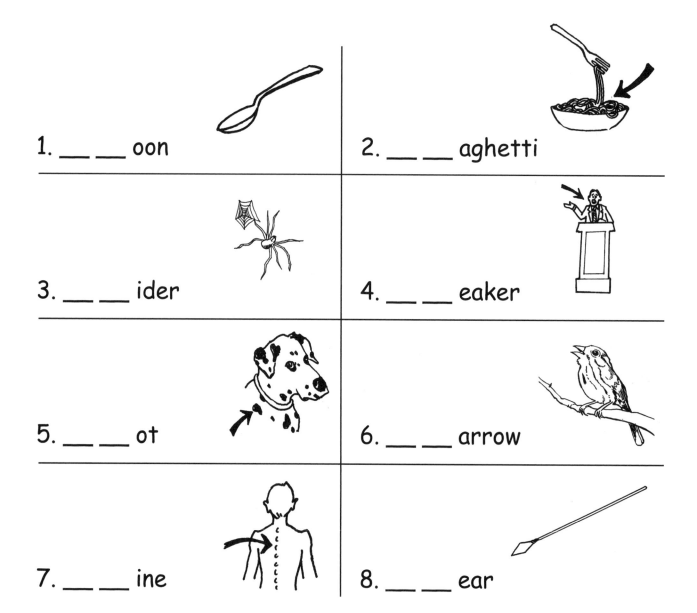

1. __ __ oon

2. __ __ aghetti

3. __ __ ider

4. __ __ eaker

5. __ __ ot

6. __ __ arrow

7. __ __ ine

8. __ __ ear

ESL Phonics for All Ages Book 3 · © Elizabeth Claire, Inc. 2008

👂 Listen, 🐞 Say, and ✏️ Write

👂 Listen to the words.

🐞 Say the words.

✏️ Write **sm** at the beginning of the words.

1. __ __ oke

2. __ __ ile

3. __ __ ell

4. __ __ udge

5. __ __ ock

👂 Listen, 🕷Say, and ✏ Write

👂 Listen to the words. 🕷 Say the words.

✏ Write the letters **st, sp, or sm.**

1. __ __ ar

2. __ __ oon

3. __ __ ider

4. __ __ ove

5. __ __ oke

6. __ __ ile

7. __ __ udent

8. __ __ ot

UNIT 3

⌒ Listen, Say, and ✎ Write

⌒ Listen to the words.

🐝 Say the words.

✎ Write **sk** at the beginning of these words.

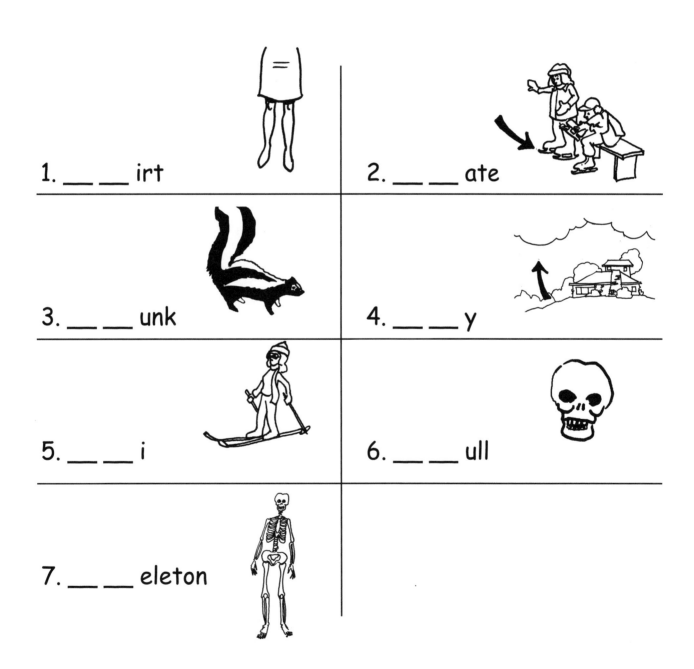

1. __ __ irt

2. __ __ ate

3. __ __ unk

4. __ __ y

5. __ __ i

6. __ __ ull

7. __ __ eleton

👂 Listen, 😊 Say, and ✏️ Write

👂 Listen to the words.

😊 Say the words.

✏️ Write **sn** at the beginning of these words.

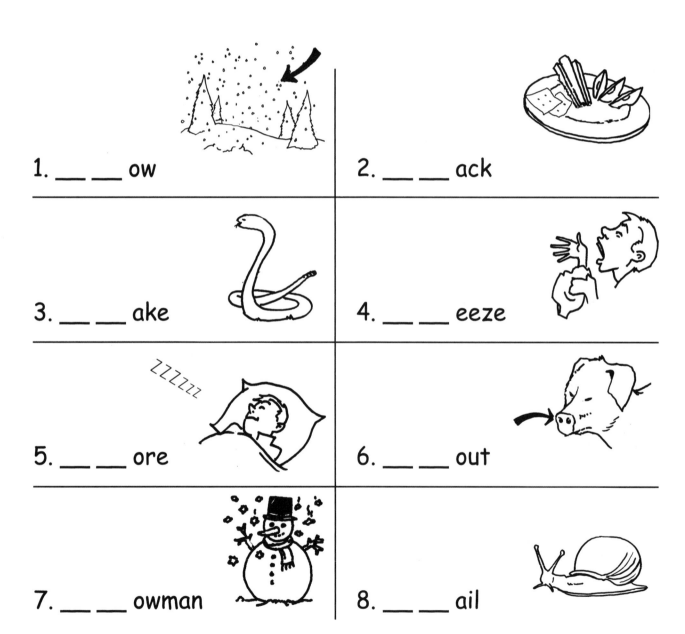

1. __ __ ow

2. __ __ ack

3. __ __ ake

4. __ __ eeze

5. __ __ ore

6. __ __ out

7. __ __ owman

8. __ __ ail

👂 Listen, 🐞 Say, and ✏️ Write

👂 Listen to the words.

🐞 Say the words.

✏️ Write **SW** at the beginning of these words.

1. __ __ eater

2. __ __ an

3. __ __ im

4. __ __ eat

5. __ __ eep

6. __ __ ing

7. __ __ itch

👂 Listen, 🗣 Say, and ✏ Write

👂 Listen to the words. 🗣 Say the words.

✏ Write the letters **sk, sn,** or **sw**.

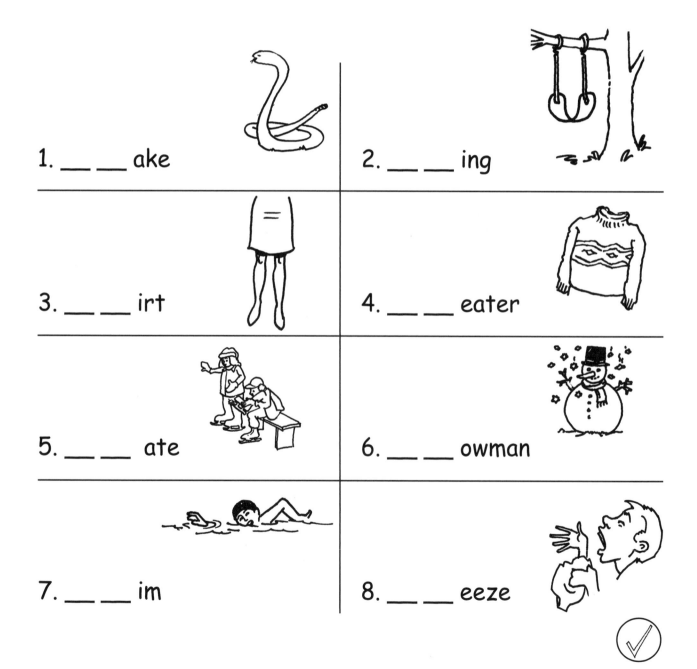

1. __ __ ake

2. __ __ ing

3. __ __ irt

4. __ __ eater

5. __ __ ate

6. __ __ owman

7. __ __ im

8. __ __ eeze

UNIT 3

Look at the pictures.   Listen to the sentences.

Find the correct sentence.

1.

a. They will stand on the steps.

b. They will swing.

2.

a. They will skate on the stove.

b. They will ski in the snow.

3.

a. They will smell the skunk.

b. They will sweep the snail.

4.

a. They will run from the snake.

b. They will sneeze at the swan.

UNIT 3   39

Puzzle: Read and ○ Find

Read the words. ○ Find the words in the puzzle.

✎ Draw a line around the words in the puzzle.

blouse   prize   spoon

brush   smile   spot

crib   sneeze   star

frog   snack   step

glove   snowman   swan

a	b	c	b	r	u	s	h	d	e
f	s	t	a	r	s	p	o	o	n
s	n	a	c	k	g	o	h	i	j
k	o	f	l	y	s	t	e	p	b
s	w	a	n	l	k	c	m	r	l
s	m	i	l	e	i	r	n	i	o
b	a	m	b	c	d	i	r	z	u
s	n	e	e	z	e	b	v	e	s
t	u	f	r	o	g	l	o	v	e

Read, Find, and Circle

Read the words.

Find two words that are the same.

Draw a circle around the same words.

1. stamp	snack	skirt	skunk	snack

2. swan	swim	snore	sweat	snore

3. smoke	smell	smell	spoon	stamp

4. skirt	skunk	skirt	stair	star

5. snow	swan	snore	sweat	swan

6. spider	sweater	skirt	spoon	spider

Listen, 👓 Say, and ✏ Write

👂 Listen to the words.

👓 Say the words.

✏ Write **sk, sl, sm, sn, sp, st, or sw**.

1. __ __ eep	2. __ __ ile	3. __ __ eeve
4. __ __ ot	5. __ __ oon	6. __ __ ar
7. __ __ ove	8. __ __ eleton	9. __ __ irt
10. __ __ oke	11. __ __ eeze	12. __ __ ake
13. __ __ ore	14. __ __ in	15. __ __ eep
16. __ __ art	17. __ __ im	18. __ __ ow
19. __ __ atue	20. __ __ em	21. __ __ eak

UNIT 3

ESL Phonics for All Ages Book 3 · © Elizabeth Claire, Inc. 2008

👂 Listen, 🗣 Say, and ✏ Write

These words begin with the sounds /tr/.

👂 Listen to the words.   🗣 Say the words.

✏ Write **tr** at the beginning of these words.

1. __ __ ee

2. __ __ ain

3. __ __ ay

4. __ __ acks

5. __ __ uck

6. __ __ ash

7. __ __ ap

8. __ __ ophy

👂 Listen, 🕷️ Say, and ✏️ Write

These words begin with the sounds /tw/.

👂 Listen to the words. 🕷️ Say the words.

✏️ Write **tw** at the beginning of these words.

1. __ __ ins

2. __ __ enty   **20**

3. __ __ elve   **12**

4. __ __ eezers

5. __ __ inkle

6. __ __ ig

ESL Phonics for All Ages Book 3 · © Elizabeth Claire, Inc. 2008

👂 Listen, 🗣 Say, and ✏️ Write

These words begin with the sound /thr/.

👂 Listen to the words.　🗣 Say the words.

✏️ Write **thr** at the beginning of these words.

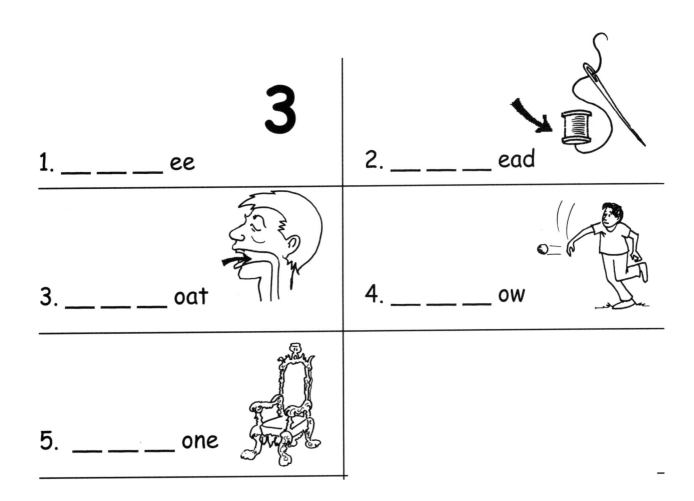

3

1. __ __ __ __ ee

2. __ __ __ __ ead

3. __ __ __ __ oat

4. __ __ __ __ ow

5. __ __ __ __ one

👂 Listen, 😛 Say, and ✏️ Write

👂 Listen to the words.

😛 Say the words.

✏️ Write **SC** at the beginning of these words.

1. __ __ arf

2. __ __ oop

3. __ __ alp

4. __ __ ar

5. __ __ uba diver

6. __ __ ale

7. __ __ hool

8. __ __ ore

YOU	ME
ⅢⅢ Ⅰ	Ⅲ

👂 Listen, 😀 Say, and ✏ Write

👂 Listen to the words. 😀 Say the words.

✏ Write **tr, tw, thr**, or **sc** at the beginning of these words.

3

1. __ __ uck

2. __ __ ale

3. __ __ __ ee

4. __ __ ee

5. __ __ ain

6. __ __ hool

7. __ __ ins

8. __ __ arf

Twinkle, Twinkle, Little Star

Twinkle, twinkle, little star,

How I wonder what you are.

Up above the world so high,

Like a diamond in the sky;
Twinkle, twinkle, little star,

How I wonder
what you are!

48

UNIT 4

👂 Listen, 🕷Say, and ✏ Write

👂 Listen to the words.

🕷 Say the words.

✏ Write **tr, tw, sc, st,** or **sn**.

1. __ __ inkle

2. __ __ arf

3. __ __ ake

4. __ __ ain

5. __ __ ins

6. __ __ ack

7. __ __ hool

8. __ __ uck

9. __ __ elve

10. __ __ enty

11. __ __ ash

12. __ __ ap

13. __ __ ale

14. __ __ ore

15. __ __ acks

16. __ __ eezers

17. __ __ ar

18. __ __ oop

19. __ __ ay

20. __ __ ophy

21. __ __ ig

👂 Listen, 🗣 Say, and ✏ Write

👂 Listen to the words.

🗣 Say the words.

✏ Write **scr** at the beginning of these words.

1. __ __ __ eam

2. __ __ __ ew

3. __ __ __ ub

4. __ __ __ een

5. __ __ __ ap book

6. __ __ __ ipt

abcd

7. __ __ __ ibble

👂 Listen, 🐞 Say, and ✏️ Write

👂 Listen to the words.

🐞 Say the words.

✏️ Write **spl** at the beginning of these words.

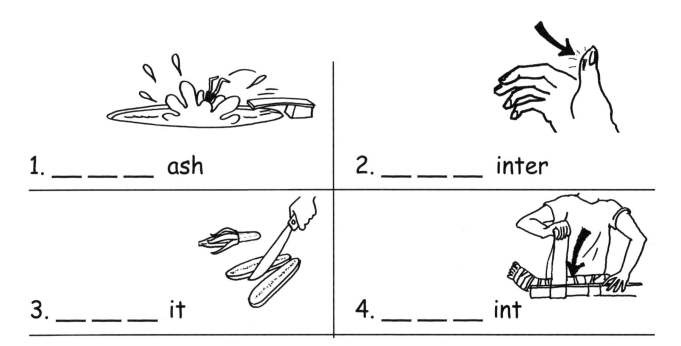

1. __ __ __ ash

2. __ __ __ inter

3. __ __ __ it

4. __ __ __ int

👂 Listen, 🐜 Say, and ✏ Write

👂 Listen to the words.

🐜 Say the words.

✏ Write **spr** at the beginning of these words.

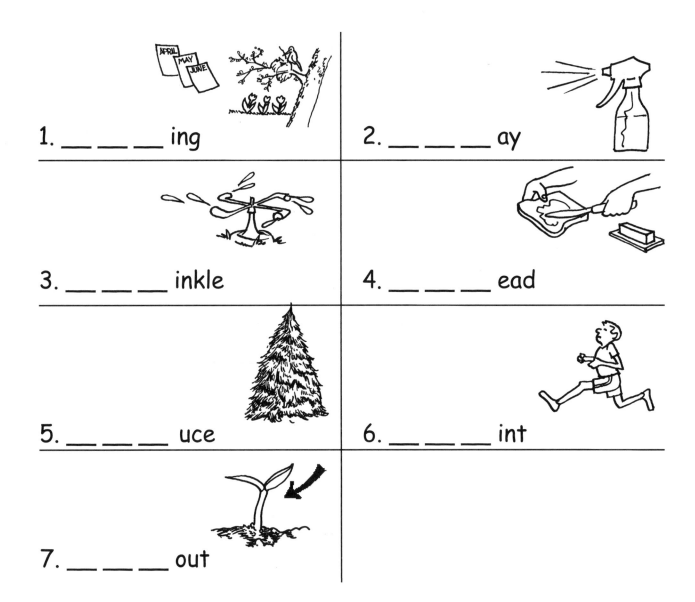

1. __ __ __ __ ing

2. __ __ __ __ ay

3. __ __ __ __ inkle

4. __ __ __ __ ead

5. __ __ __ __ uce

6. __ __ __ __ int

7. __ __ __ __ out

(ear) Listen, (face) Say, and (pencil) Write

(ear) Listen to the words.

(face) Say the words.

(pencil) Write **squ** at the beginning of these words.

1. _ _ _ are

2. _ _ _ _ irrel

3. _ _ _ ash

4. _ _ _ _ eeze

5. _ _ _ _ id

6. _ _ _ _ at

7. _ _ _ int

👂 Listen, 🐞 Say, and ✏️ Write

👂 Listen to the words.

🐞 Say the words.

✏️ Write **str** at the beginning of these words.

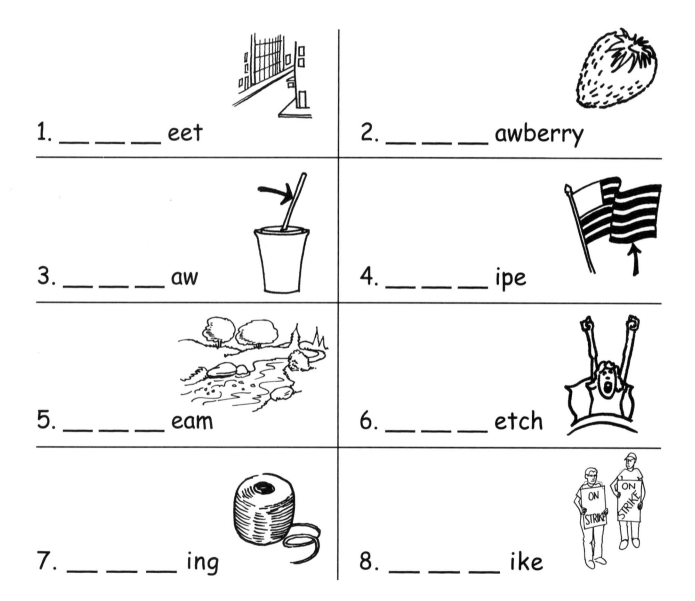

1. _ _ _ _ eet

2. _ _ _ _ awberry

3. _ _ _ _ aw

4. _ _ _ _ ipe

5. _ _ _ _ eam

6. _ _ _ _ etch

7. _ _ _ _ ing

8. _ _ _ _ ike

Find and Circle

Read the words.

Find two words that are the same.

Draw a circle around the same words.

1. square   stairs   street   squirrel   street
---
2. splash   squash   squint   screw   squash
---
3. scrub   scratch   scrub   sprint   spring
---
4. spread   script   sprout   scrub   sprout
---
5. sprinkle   spring   squirrel   spring   squash
---
6. spray   straw   stripe   stripe   string

👂 Listen, 🐜 Say, and ✏️ Write

👂 Listen to the words.

🐜 Say the words.

✏️ Write **scr, squ, str,** or **thr**.

1. __ __ __ awberry

2. __ __ __ are

3. __ __ __ ub

4. __ __ __ irrel

5. __ __ __ ipes

6. __ __ __ ee

7. __ __ __ eet

8. __ __ __ ow

UNIT 5

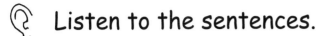 Listen and Read

 Look at the pictures.

 Listen to the sentences.

 Read the sentences.  Find the correct sentence.

1.
a. He will scream at the squirrel.

b. He will squeeze the strawberry.

2.
a. He will squirt the squirrel!

b. He will sprinkle the square.

3.
a. He will scrub the square.

b. He will throw the throne.

4.
a. He will splash in the street.

b. He will stretch the string.

👂 Listen, 🗣 Say, and ✏ Write

👂 Listen to the words. 🗣 Say the words.

✏ Write **scr, spr, str, squ,** or **thr**.

1. __ __ __ are

2. __ __ __ eet

3. __ __ __ ing

4. __ __ __ one

5. __ __ __ irrel

6. __ __ __ awberry

7. __ __ __ ipe

8. __ __ __ are

9. __ __ __ ow

10. __ __ __ eam

11. __ __ __ ead

12. __ __ __ ead

13. __ __ __ ong

14. __ __ __ eam

15. __ __ __ ing

16. __ __ __ ee

I scream,

You scream,

We all scream

For ice cream!

👂 Listen, 😋 Say, and ✏️ Write

👂 Listen to the words.   😋 Say the words.

✏️ Write **st** at the end of these words.

1. toa ___ ___	2. ne ___ ___
3. fi ___ ___	4. ca ___ ___
5. ve ___ ___	6. te ___ ___
7. wri ___ ___	8. gho ___ ___

👂 Listen, 🐜 Say, and ✏️ Write

👂 Listen to the words. 🐜 Say the words.

✏️ Write **nt** at the end of these words.

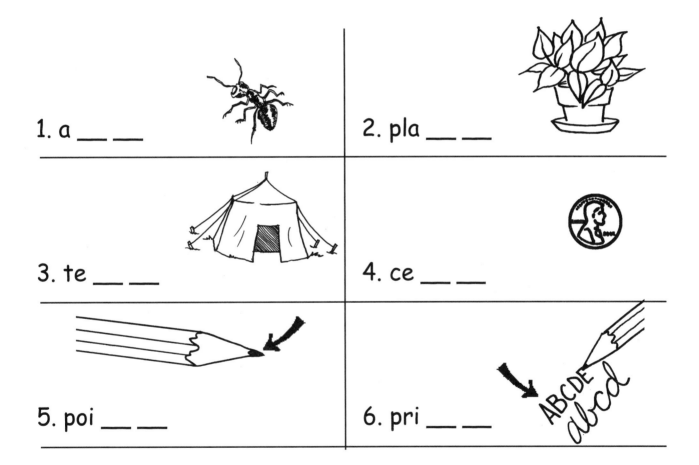

1. a __ __

2. pla __ __

3. te __ __

4. ce __ __

5. poi __ __

6. pri __ __

👂 Listen, 🐜 Say, and ✏️ Write

👂 Listen to the words.　🐜　Say the words.

✏️ Write **ft** at the end of these words.

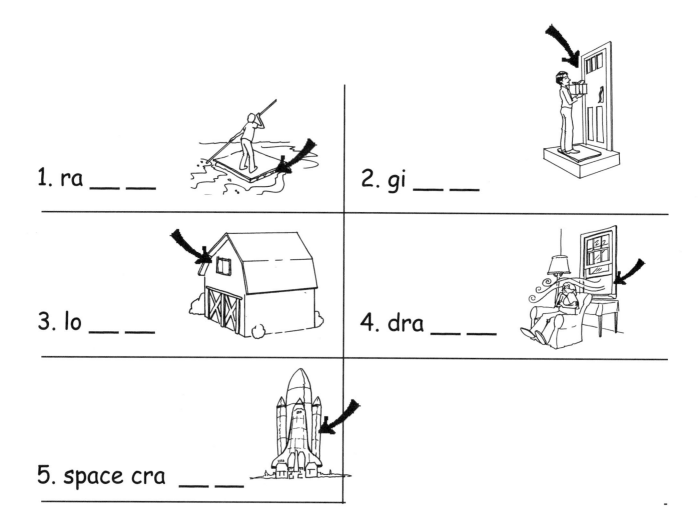

1. ra __ __

2. gi __ __

3. lo __ __

4. dra __ __

5. space cra __ __

UNIT 6

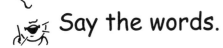 Listen, 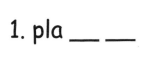 Say, and ✎ Write

👂 Listen to the words.

🐞 Say the words.

✎ Write **st, nt,** or **ft**.

1. pla __ __ 	2. toa __ __ 
3. gi __ __ 	4. te __ __ 
5. ra __ __ 	6. a __ __
7. fi __ __ 	8. ne __ __ 

 **Find, and Circle**

 Look at the words.

 Find two words that are the same.

Draw a circle around the same words.

1. tent	toast	plant	toast	fist

2. gift	test	raft	nest	raft

3. print	plant	draft	soft	plant

4. raft	gift	lift	left	lift

5. vest	wrist	vest	test	nest

6. count	hunt	fist	ant	ant

UNIT 6

ESL Phonics for All Ages Book 3 · © Elizabeth Claire, Inc. 2008

👂 Listen, 🐞 Say, and ✏️ Write

These words end with the sounds /nk/.

👂 Listen to the words. 🐞 Say the words.

✏️ Write the letters **nk** in these words.

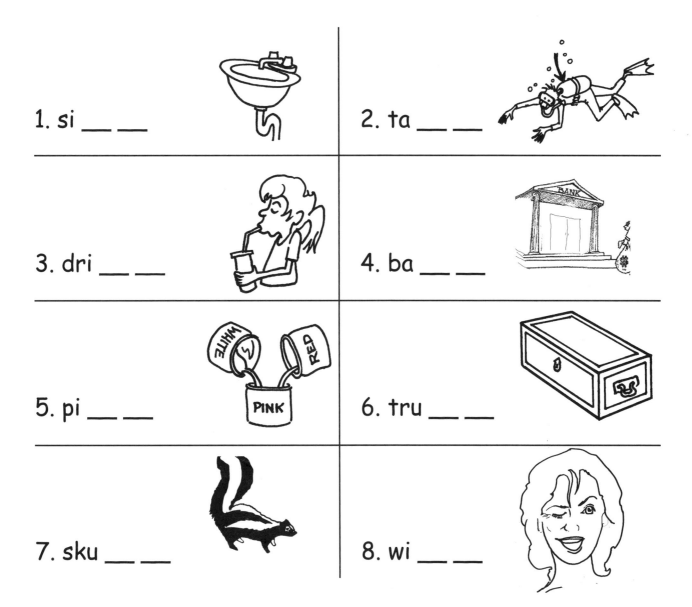

1. si __ __

2. ta __ __

3. dri __ __

4. ba __ __

5. pi __ __

6. tru __ __

7. sku __ __

8. wi __ __

👂 Listen, 🗣 Say, and ✏ Write

👂 Listen to the words.

🗣 Say the words.

✏ Write **nd** in these words.

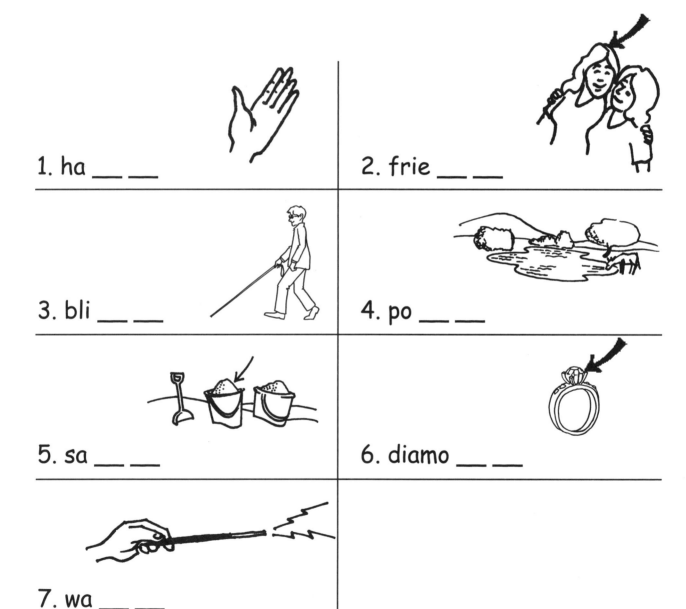

1. ha __ __

2. frie __ __

3. bli __ __

4. po __ __

5. sa __ __

6. diamo __ __

7. wa __ __

Listen, Say, and Write

Listen to the words.

Say the words.

Write **mp** in these words.

1. la __ __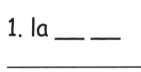

2. ju __ __

3. sta __ __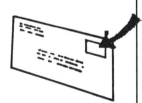

4. gas pu __ __

5. bu __ __

6. hu __ __

7. shri __ __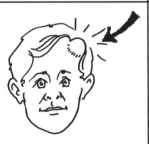

8. stu __ __

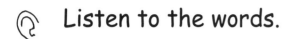 Listen,  Say, and ✎ Write

 Listen to the words.

 Say the words.

✎ Write **nk, nd,** or **mp**.

1. frie __ __

2. sku __ __

3. si __ __

4. ju __ __

5. ha __ __

6. sta __ __

7. la __ __

8. diamo __ __

UNIT 6

ESL Phonics for All Ages Book 3 · © Elizabeth Claire, Inc. 2008

The Bear Went Over the Mountain

The bear went over the mountain,
The bear went over the mountain,
The bear went over the mountain,
To see what he could see.

And what do you think he saw?
And what do you think he saw?

The other side of the mountain,
The other side of the mountain,
The other side of the mountain,
Was all that he could see.

UNIT 6

👂 Listen, 🗣️ Say, and ✏️ Write

👓 Look at the pictures. 👂 Listen to the words.

🗣️ Say the words.

✏️ Write **le** in these words.

1. bicyc __ __ 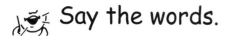	2. icic __ __
3. circ __ __	4. bubb __ __
5. puzz __ __	6. turt __ __
7. bott __ __	8. jugg __ __

ESL Phonics for All Ages Book 3 · © Elizabeth Claire, Inc. 2008

👂 Listen, 🗣 Say, and ✏ Write

👓 Look at the pictures.   👂 Listen to the words.

🗣 Say the words.

✏ Write **le** in these words.

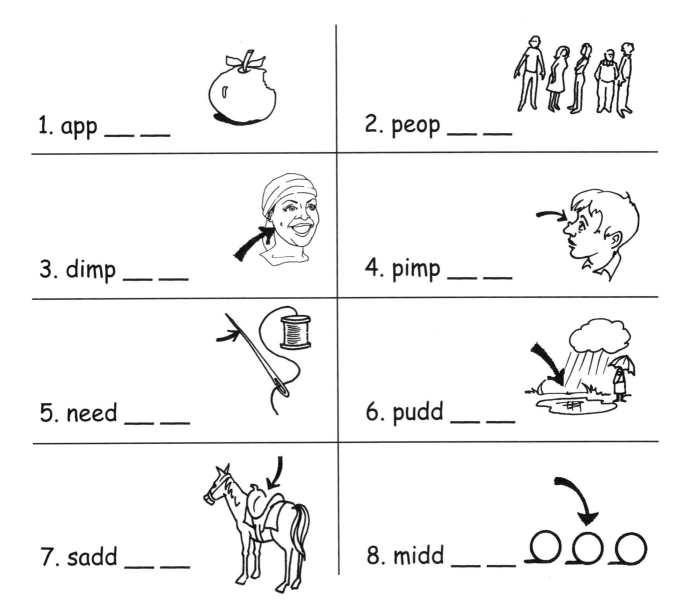

1. app __ __

2. peop __ __

3. dimp __ __

4. pimp __ __

5. need __ __

6. pudd __ __

7. sadd __ __

8. midd __ __

👂 Listen, 🐜 Say, and ✏️ Write

👓 Look at the pictures.   👂 Listen to the words.

🐜 Say the words.

✏️ Write **le** in these words.

1. cand __ __

2. kett __ __

3. tab __ __

4. whist __ __

5. padd __ __

6. buck __ __

7. musc __ __

8. ank __ __

UNIT 7

Puzzle: Read and ◯ Find

 Read the words.   ◯Find the words in the puzzle.

 Draw a circle around the words in the puzzle.

apple	little	people
bicycle	middle	puddle
bottle	needle	saddle
bubble	noodle	title
circle	paddle	turtle
juggle		

a	a	p	p	l	e	b	n	o	o	d	l	e
b	c	e	b	u	b	b	l	e	d	i	p	e
o	c	o	f	t	i	t	l	e	j	m	u	m
t	i	p	g	u	c	h	i	j	u	p	d	i
t	r	l	k	r	y	l	m	n	g	l	d	d
l	c	e	o	t	c	p	q	r	g	e	l	d
e	l	s	t	l	l	i	t	t	l	e	e	l
u	e	v	n	e	e	d	l	e	e	w	x	e
y	p	a	d	d	l	e	s	a	d	d	l	e

👓 Look and 🔍 Find

👓 Look at the pictures. 👂 Listen to the sentences.

🔍 Find the correct sentence.

1.

    a. There is an apple in the bottle.

    b. There is a candle on the table.

2.

    a. There is a turtle in a puddle.

    b. There is a buckle on the saddle

3.

    a. There is a kettle on the stove.

    b. There is a noodle on a bicycle.

4.

    a. There is a dimple on her cheek.

    b. There is a pimple on her nose.

👂 Listen, 🗣 Say, and ✏ Write

👂 Listen to the words. 🗣 Say the words.

✏ Write **ft, le, mp, nd, nk, nt, nk,** or **st**.

1. bott __ __	2. poi __ __	3. si __ __
4. gho__ __	5. bubb __ __	6. ha __ __
7. pla __ __	8. kett __ __	9. gi __ __
10. app __ __	11. sa __ __	12. sta __ __
13. tru __ __	14. dra __ __	15. pu __ __
16. ank __ __	17. toa __ __	18. te __ __
19. ta __ __	20. peop __ __	21. need __ __

👂 Listen, 🐞Say, and ✏️ Write

👂 Listen to the words. 🐞 Say the words.

✏️ Write **b, t,** or **m** in the <u>middle</u> of these words.

1. ba __ y

2. wo__ an

3. po __ ato

4. volley __ all

5. fa __ ily

6. ar __ ist

7. el __ ow

8. to __ ato

👂 Listen, 🗣 Say, and ✏ Write

👂   Listen to the words.

🗣   Say the words.

✏   Write **k, p,** or **d** in the middle of these words.

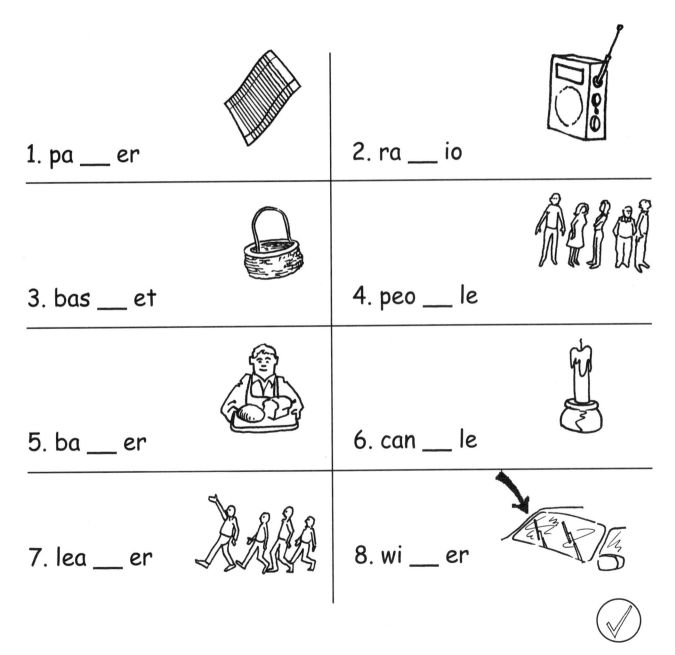

1. pa __ er

2. ra __ io

3. bas __ et

4. peo __ le

5. ba __ er

6. can __ le

7. lea __ er

8. wi __ er

👂 Listen, 🗣 Say, and ✏ Write

👂 Listen to the words.

🗣 Say the words.

✏ Write **n, v,** or **s** in the middle of these words.

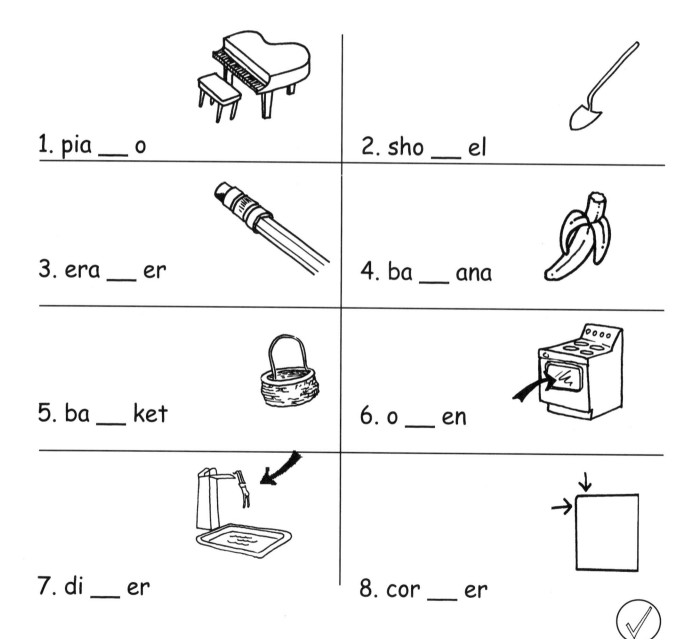

1. pia ___ o

2. sho ___ el

3. era ___ er

4. ba ___ ana

5. ba ___ ket

6. o ___ en

7. di ___ er

8. cor ___ er

✓

UNIT **8**

ESL Phonics for All Ages Book 3 · © Elizabeth Claire, Inc. 2008

👂 Listen, 🗣 Say, and ✏ Write

👂 Listen to the words.

🗣 Say the words.

✏ Write **g, l,** or **x** in the middle of these words.

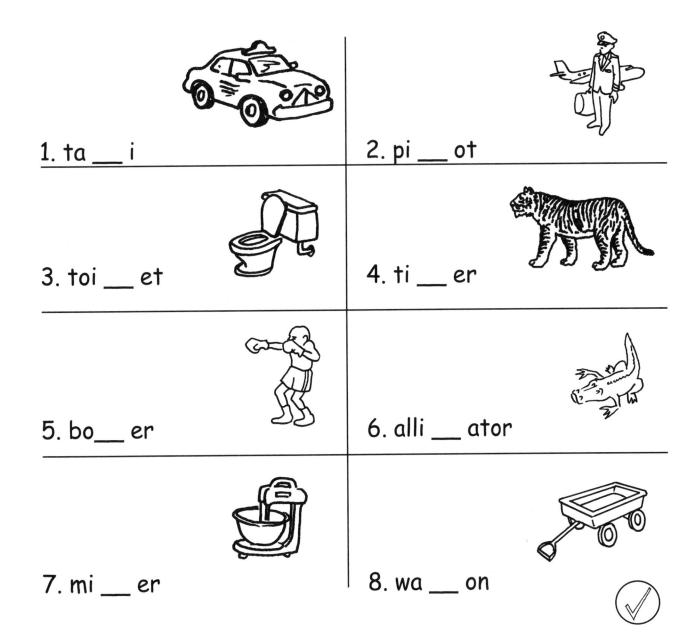

1. ta ___ i

2. pi ___ ot

3. toi ___ et

4. ti ___ er

5. bo ___ er

6. alli ___ ator

7. mi ___ er

8. wa ___ on

👂 Listen, 🗣 Say, and ✏️ Write

👂 Listen to the words. 🗣 Say the words.

✏️ Write **ch, sh,** or **th** in the middle of these words.

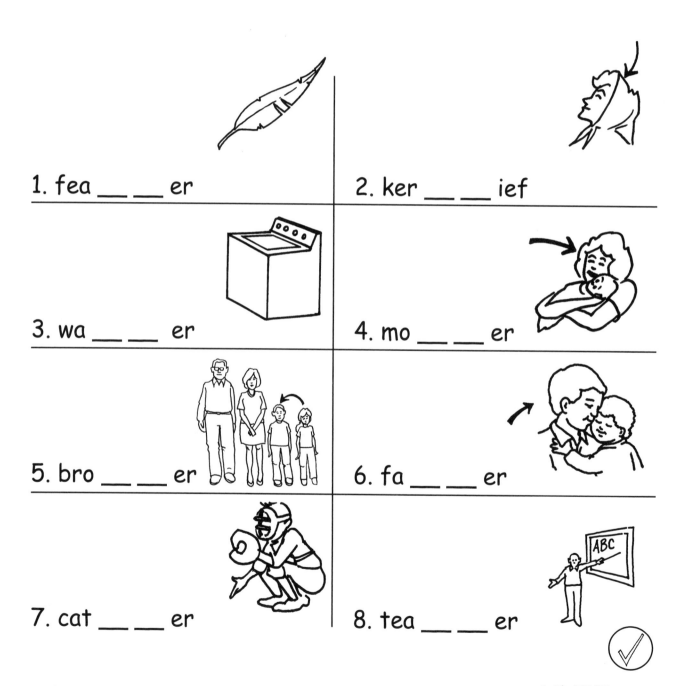

1. fea __ __ er

2. ker __ __ ief

3. wa __ __ er

4. mo __ __ er

5. bro __ __ er

6. fa __ __ er

7. cat __ __ er

8. tea __ __ er

UNIT 8

ESL Phonics for All Ages Book 3 · © Elizabeth Claire, Inc. 2008

👂 Listen, 🗣 Say, and ✏ Write

👂 Listen to the words. 🗣 Say the words.

✏ Write **bb, dd, ll, mm,** or **zz** in the middle of these words.

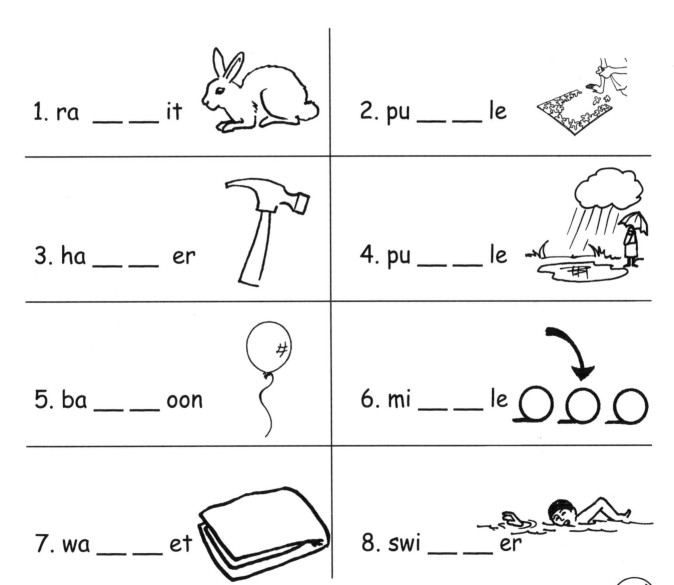

1. ra __ __ it

2. pu __ __ le

3. ha __ __ er

4. pu __ __ le

5. ba __ __ oon

6. mi __ __ le

7. wa __ __ et

8. swi __ __ er

👂 Listen, 🗣 Say, and ✏ Write

👂 Listen to the words. 🗣 Say the words.

✏ Write **ff, rr, pp,** or **tt** in the middle of these words.

1. zi ___ ___ er	2. ca ___ ___ ot
3. le ___ ___ er	4. co ___ ___ ee
5. mu ___ ___ in	6. a ___ ___ le
7. mi ___ ___ ens	8. mi ___ ___ or

UNIT 8

ESL Phonics for All Ages Book 3 · © Elizabeth Claire, Inc. 2008

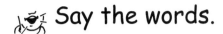 **Listen,** **Say, and** ✏ **Write**

👓 Look at the pictures. 👂 Listen to the words.

 Say the words.

✏ Write two letters in the middle of these words.

1. sa __ __ wich

2. foo __ __ all

3. ba __ __ et

4. bli __ __ er

5. mo __ __ ey

6. ze __ __ a

7. mai __ __ ox

8. whi __ __ er

Listen and Read the Story
The Grasshopper and the Ants

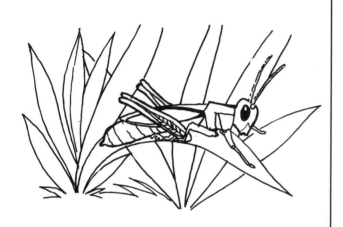

1. A grasshopper loved to play. He played all summer. He had plenty of grass to eat.

2. He saw many little ants. They were bringing food to their nest under the ground.

3. "Hello Grasshopper," said an ant. "It's time to work, not play. Winter is coming.

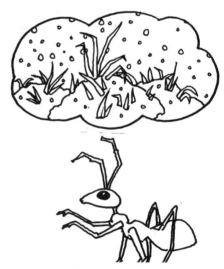

4. It will be cold. The grass will die. The land will be frozen. There will be no food."

84

The Grasshopper and the Ants: 2

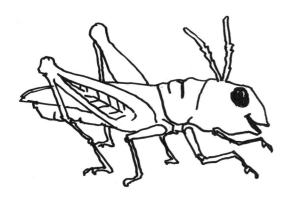

5. "Ha ha," said the grass-hopper. "I don't like to work. I like to play."

6. Soon, winter came. It was cold. The grass died. The land was frozen.

7. The ants were in their nest under the ground. They had plenty of food.

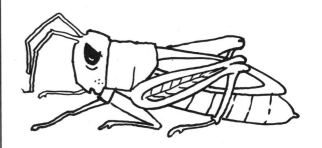

8. The grasshopper was cold and hungry. He had nothing to eat.

UNIT 9

85

9. He went to the ants' nest. "Hello, little ants," said the grasshopper.

10. "I am hungry. I am cold. Can I come in to your warm house? Can I have some food to eat?"

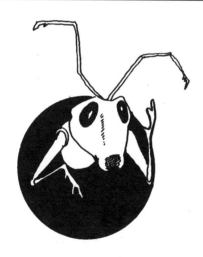

11. "We are so sorry," said the ant. "We don't have food for you. We only have food for ants.

12. When we worked, you played. Now we will play." The little ants closed the door.

The Grasshopper and the Ants: 4

grasshopper   ants

food   nest

grass   winter

Read the sentences.

Draw a circle around the best word.

1. The grasshopper loved to _____.

    (work   play)

2. The grasshopper played all _____.

    (summer   winter)

3. The grasshopper had plenty of _____
    to eat.

    (glass   grass)

The Grasshopper and the Ants: 5

 Read the sentences.

Draw a circle around the best word.

4. The little _____ worked all summer.

   (plants   ants)

5. The ants were bringing food to their _____.

   (nest   neck)

6. Winter came. The _____ was cold and hungry.

   (ant   grasshopper)

7. The grasshopper went to the ants' house. "Can I
   have some _____ to eat?" he said.

   (flood   food)

8. "We are sorry," said the ants. "We don't have

   food for you. When we worked, you played. Now

   we will _____.

   (play   work)

UNIT 9

ESL Phonics for All Ages Book 3 · © Elizabeth Claire, Inc. 2008

The Grasshopper and the Ants: 6

Who said it, the grasshopper or the ants?
Draw a circle around the best word.

1. "Winter is coming."   grasshopper   ants

2. "I don't like to work."   grasshopper   ants

3. "I am cold and hungry."   grasshopper   ants

4. "Can I have some food to eat?"

                                                         grasshopper   ants

5. "We don't have food for you."

                                                         grasshopper   ants

6. "Now we will play."   grasshopper   ants

The Grasshopper and the Ants: 7

What happened first? What happened next?

✏ Write 1, 2, 3, 4 and 5 in the correct order.

_____ Winter came. The grass died.

_____ The ants closed their door.

__1__ The grasshopper played all summer.

_____ The grasshopper was hungry.

_____ The grasshopper went to the ants' nest.

ESL Phonics for All Ages Book 3 · © Elizabeth Claire, Inc. 2008

Review 1: Beginning Consonant Clusters

Listen to the words.　　Say the words.

Write two letters at the beginning of these words.

1. __ __ oset　2. __ __ ant　3. __ __ ower

4. __ __ ane　5. __ __ eep　6. __ __ anket

7. __ __ ize　8. __ __ ush　9. __ __ iend

10. __ __ ive　11. __ __ ar　12. __ __ ayons

13. __ __ oke　14. __ __ irt　15. __ __andmother

16. __ __ uck　17. __ __ ake　18. __ __ aghetti

19. __ __ enty 20. __ __ ain　21. __ __ eater

Review 2: Beginning Consonant Clusters

Listen to the words.   Say the words.

Write three letters at the beginning of these words.

1. __ __ __ ub

2. __ __ __ ash

3. __ __ __ ing

4. __ __ __ awberry

5. __ __ __ irrel

6. __ __ __ are

7. __ __ __ eet

8. __ __ __ inkle

9. __ __ __ ipe

10. __ __ __ int

UNIT 10

ESL Phonics for All Ages Book 3 · © Elizabeth Claire, Inc. 2008

Review 3: Ending Consonant Clusters

Listen to the words.   Say the words.

Write two letters at the end of these words.

1. ne __ __   2. pla __ __   3. gi __ __

4. app __ __   5. hu __ __   6. ju __ __

7. bott __ __   8. sku __ __   9. frie __ __

10. toa __ __   11. peop __ __   12. cou __ __

13. si __ __   14. nood __ __   15. le __ __

16. dri __ __   17. sta __ __   18. midd __ __

Word List: New Words in Book 3

above
alligator
ant
ants
apple

baker
bank
basket
bear
bells
bicycle
black
blanket
blend
blimp
blind
blister
block
blouse
bottle
boxer
braids
brain
branch
break
bring
broom
brother
bubble
bump

came
candle
carrot
cast
catcher
clap
claws
close
closed
closet
clothes
cloud
clown

coffee
cold
coming
consonant
corner
count
crab
crayons
crow
crowd
crown
cry

diamond
die
died
dimple
ding
diver
don't
dong
draft
dragon
drapes
drawer
drive

end
eraser

feather
fist
flame
flea
flood
floor
flute
food
for
fractions
frame
freeze
Friday

friend
frozen
fruit
fry

ghost
gift
glasses
globe
glove
glue
grandfather
grandmother
grapes
grasshopper
grave
green
grocery store
ground

ha ha
hammer
hands
high
hump
hungry
hunt

ice cream
icicle
if

John
juggle
jump

kerchief

land
leader

left
letter
lift
little
loft
loved

many
middle
mirror
mixer
morning
mountain

needle
nothing

on
only
other
ought
oven

pass
people
piano
pilot
pimple
pink
plaid
plane
planet
plant
plate
plenty
pliers
plug
plus
point
pond
pound
pray

94

present	slap	squaw	trash
pretzel	sled	squeeze	tray
price	sleep	squint	tree
prince	sleeping	squirrel	trophy
print	sleeve	squirt	trunk
prison	slide	stairs	turkey
prize	slipper	stamp	turtle
prune	smart	stand	tweezers
puddle	smell	star	twelve
pump	smile	step	twig
	smock	stick	twine
	smoke	stove	twinkle
raft	smudge	stranger	
really	snack	straw	
ringing	snail	strawberry	under
	snake	stretch	
	sneeze	strike	
saddle	snore	string	wagon
sand	snout	stripe	wand
scale	snow	student	was
scalp	snowman	stump	washer
scar	so	summer	whisper
scarf	soft	swallow	wink
scoop	sorry	swan	winter
score	space craft	sweat	wiper
scorpion	spaghetti	sweater	won't
scrap book	sparrow	sweep	wonder
scratch	speak	swim	work
scream	spear	swimmer	world
screen	spider	switch	wrist
screw	spine		
scribble	splash		you're
script	splint	tank	
scrub	splinter	tent	
show	split	think	
shrimp	spoon	thread	
side	spot	three	
sink	spray	throat	
skate	spread	throne	
skeleton	spring	throw	
ski	sprinkle	tiger	
skirt	sprout	time	
skull	spruce	toast	
skunk	square	tracks	
sky	squash	train	
slacks	squat	trap	

My Work

Check your work.
Write the number correct next to the page number.

Page	Correct / Total		Page	Correct / Total		Page	Correct / Total
8	_____ / 8		40	_____ / 15		76	_____ / 8
9	_____ / 6		41	_____ / 6		77	_____ / 8
10	_____ / 4		42	_____ / 21		78	_____ / 8
15	_____ / 8		47	_____ / 8		79	_____ / 8
16	_____ / 6		49	_____ / 21		80	_____ / 8
20	_____ / 8		55	_____ / 6		81	_____ / 8
21	_____ / 6		56	_____ / 8		82	_____ / 8
25	_____ / 6		57	_____ / 4		83	_____ / 8
26	_____ / 8		58	_____ / 16		87/88	_____ / 8
28	_____ / 8		63	_____ / 8		89	_____ / 6
29	_____ / 4		64	_____ / 6		90	_____ / 5
30	_____ / 21		68	_____ / 8		91	_____ / 21
34	_____ / 8		73	_____ / 16		92	_____ / 10
38	_____ / 8		74	_____ / 4		93	_____ / 18
39	_____ / 4		75	_____ / 21			

ESL Phonics for All Ages Book 3 · © Elizabeth Claire, Inc. 2008